Boudicca & Co.

JANE HOLLAND is an English poet, novelist, editor and former professional snooker player, born in Essex in 1966. She won an Eric Gregory Award for her poetry in 1996. Her first collection, *The Brief History of a Disreputable Woman*, was published by Bloodaxe in 1997. A first novel, *Kissing the Pink*, followed from Sceptre in 1999. One of the top poetry performers in the Midlands, she currently lives in Warwickshire with her husband and five children.

Also by Jane Holland

POETRY
The Brief History of a Disreputable Woman (Bloodaxe, 1997)

FICTION
Kissing the Pink (Sceptre, 1999)

Boudicca & Co.

JANE HOLLAND

SALT

CAMBRIDGE

PUBLISHED BY SALT PUBLISHING
PO Box 937, Great Wilbraham, Cambridge PDO CB1 5JX United Kingdom

© Jane Holland, 2006

The right of Jane Holland to be identified as the
author of this work has been asserted by her in accordance
with Section 77 of the Copyright, Designs and Patents Act 1988.

Salt Publishing 2006

Printed and bound in the United States of America by Lightning Source

Typeset in Swift 9.5 / 13

ISBN-13 978 1 84471 289 2 paperback
ISBN-10 1 84471 289 3 paperback

SP

1 3 5 7 9 8 6 4 2

For Steve Haynes

Contents

'The structure of all poetry is the movement that an active individuality makes in expressing itself. Poetic rhythm, of which we have all spoken so much, is the chart of a temperament.'

MINA LOY, from 'MODERN POETRY',
an essay in *Lost Lunar Baedaker* (1996/97)

Acknowledgements

Acknowledgements are due to the editors of the following publications and webzines in which some of these poems first appeared:

Acumen, avocado, Boomerang, Brando's Hat, Isis, Limelight, The Nail, PN Review, Poetry Review, Under the Hill (Isle of Man Poetry Society).

With grateful thanks to Judy Ewart, Brendan Kennelly, Neil Rollinson, Julia Copus, David Ewart, Sophie Hannah, Roly Drower, Mark Haddon, Sos Eltis, Sebastian Barker, William Oxley and Steve Haynes for their friendship, advice and encouragement through many difficult times.

Part I

Oyster

I cruised the coast roads alone
that summer; metallic sea
was all I knew, sirocco
blowing hot and southerly.
One afternoon, sweltering
through the low gears,
I stopped the car, stared out
from my carapace
and the sirocco blew, wedging
a pearl-like piece of grit
under one stubborn eyelid,
blurring the horizon
to an accumulation of light,
a working within, to you
coming to me, triumphantly
prising open the oyster.

In Response to a Nude Photograph of Mina Loy, 1905

Women poets are not supposed to look like that,
did nobody tell you? The one
with the cigarette is bullish enough
but this, taken naked, face
against the wall with one arse cheek
suggestively raised
is the portrait of a muse, my dear.
In later years, your beauty was eclipsed by age.
Here your skin's like frost, that white back
and hourglass waist
crying out to be marked, to be photographed.
Did it feel safer like this, turned away
in your nakedness,
to be stared at, lusted after?
'Leave off looking to men to find out
what you are not,' you said.
Then let me take you to to bed, Mina,
to the ostrich feather bed
of our imagination. There we'll smoke
and make poetry all day, decadent
in our sticky love,
looking each other in the eye, drinking
each other's blood
like tea from a china dish, steeped
in what it means to be us, spawning
our poems like fish.

Hot Days in the Eighties

On hot days in the eighties, you stopped
for ices at Taunton Services. Little
did you know then, twenty-something
in the white Ford Escort Estate—
radio on full, heater too, blasting out
to keep the engine cool—the traffic jams
from Portishead to Liverpool.

That was the decade of the motorway.
You chopped your locks in the back
of the car one day, dyke-short.
Kept dental dams in the glove box,
grew the hair under your arms
to a mousey fuzz. Purchased
a map of the highways, went native.

You wore a suede jacket and a crucifix
in the 'V' of your chest, strode
like a man (and the rest). Drove
a Lancia Delta into the dirt. Years later
it was a Mercedes camper van,
seven berth, and beads, hippy skirts,
needing to get close to the earth.

These days you don't get out much,
stuck in with a husband and kids.
But the road's strong, it hauls on you
like a blackbird on the worm,
and you find excuses—friends ill,
time alone—for the grip
of the wheel, a licence to roam.

It was cool inside the chapel

It was cool inside the chapel.
Blue torpor had hung over us
for months, cyanosing
the pale edge of morning.
Here, even the kids marvelled
at Matisse, adored him.

If you thought anything
of that astonishing patina
cast over white walls
by stained glass in sunlight,
you never communicated it,
turned away, smoking
your ubiquitous cigarette.

Later, we sat contemplating
the blue mosaic of fish
in one of Braque's ceramics.
Nothing had happened.
One person had simply severed
from the other, side by side
in the brilliant aftermath.

Elementals

WEST KENNETT LONG BARROW

Stone womb under an earth belly
too ancient for light.

Rain condenses its euphoric mass
to a single blessing

filtering through
the intestinal silence of rock.

Flies cling
to the mossed edge of a crevice.

She devours their small bodies like offerings.

Once, she could hold her face
up to the moon, watch it

screw a thin silver bolt
through the heavens.

Now she eats beetles
and hunts with the night-train

passing the lit windows of women
anxious for conception.

II

ALMOST ICELAND

The house was a standing stone
on the edge of annihilation.

It sat there uncomplaining
while acres of wind

pummelled and rattled windows
and floorboards.

The sea birds shunned it. The bees
rarely came so far north.

The sheep called out to it to move
but it didn't.

It just sat there.

Its single chimney grinned up at the sky
like a maniac.

For miles around, whole islands lay down
and withered. Stones

stunted themselves in its shadow.
And always the wind

hammering for the house
to be absent.

Finally, its inhabitants packed up
and left.

The house remained,
folding its arms and gritting black teeth.

It had no intention of surrender.

The wind blew on
battering its ram's head repeatedly

against lintels and uprights

its high battle-cry
prising tiles from the roof

imploding
the senseless resistance of doorways.

III

HOLY ISLAND

Pausing
after the genuflection of causeway

salt water puckers a scar
the width of her belly

creased abdomen
folding a damp cloth into sand dunes.

Whatever she gave birth to
dragged itself beyond these coarse grasses

then sloped into wind-blear

turning its back
irascibly on civilisation.

Yet the marks remain. Twice a day
they etch themselves out

along the chevroned gold
of a mackerel stomach.

The sea staggers across here on stilts

ridiculous headdress bouncing
and swaying

exhausted by cold
yet making the pilgrimage.

After it kneels to kiss the earth
sacred light flattens sand

to a blind haze
magnetised by the crawling bodies of cars.

Bare steel hulks
dredging the sun-dust

hump-hump-hump themselves

over her consecrated skein
of striations.

IV

STONE HENGE

A perfect ice-rimmed crucible
tilts itself

against the first geometry of stars.

Vast scalded pockets of fire
empty themselves

through miraculous peepholes.

Obsidian heaven
volcanised light to this glittering sacrament

that drilled ancient fires
through the eye

suggesting bears and archers

the twin shafts
of a ceaseless plough.

Now a wind-blackened cauldron
pitches its song

through these wide openings
to weather

each isolated furnace
linked

by the furious tweak
of identification

the hot craned neck of naming.

A Basket of Air

I found my first bird's nest
sixty years ago,
upside-down hat of twigs and straw
filched from the rabbits.

Inside, a clutch of pale green eggs,
freckled and still warm,
the bird somewhere above, scolding.

Now I put a hand
to that slack empty pouch
where the eggs were
and think of all those men
who wouldn't leave one shred
for me to weave, nothing
but a basket of air.

Love Song for a Gargoyle

Speak, rain-stone,
prodigal son of the buttress,

springing like a fist
foot-first from the mother,

foothold of birds
and deluge-summoner.

Tip your black throat back
into the pitch and swell

of stone breasts, loose
the bright tide dowsing her thighs.

Not master nor mastered,
mouth-piece of frogs: sing, speak, croak

the song of the disinherited,
the loveless, the bastard.

Teach me the purity
of decadence, how it strips flesh

to a shipwreck. Place
rough hoof and tongue on it.

Up here, wind takes toll,
buffets the sky

against the bluster of stunned ground,
stone-shod and blind.

You crouch above stirred air,
stiff impetus.

Drumming your wind-heels high
over rain and river

you dance for love, drenching
the silt with shudder.

A knucklebone ladder, a cage
of faith, have climbed

to leap out from this peak,
your singing spine.

Green Man

She turns in sleep, sensing him
in the dream-time. Invisible hands
press and lift her, knowing
the word that cleans her like water.
That face on the garden wall,
those hands in her bed: stern,
laughing, invincible. They told her
it could be dangerous, loving
a god. But she wouldn't listen.
Now she has ivy in her hair, seed
on her thighs. They move
wild as foxes, inevitable as earth.

The Song of the Hare

She sang the song of the hare
and the trees responded

She sang the song of the hare
and the wind trembled

She sang the song of the hare
and the stars oscillated

She sang the song of the hare
and the earth drummed

She sang the song of the hare
and the hanged man hung

as the god in the tree
put forth branches of sorrow

and the lark climbed high
in an ecstasy of cloud

Gawain's Horse

for Colin Dick

In dreams, I see his horse again; its red eyes,
its strange oak-leaf skin. What Gawain sees
I can't tell but he wakes desperate some nights,
clawing at his face. *It should have been the King.*
We've been wandering in this forest for months,
Gawain and I, neither of us daring to admit
we're lost. The year is nearly up; he babbles
in Scots in his sleep, prays for deliverance.

Morning. The road takes us again, my hooves
scoured by snow and blackened ice, burnt
like old pots on the fire. I try not to remember
the tales they told for months before we left,
the grin of the axe, its shiver of steel through bone,
grease and sinew, the head rolling and rolling
like a football, those bruised eyelids flickering
back afterwards, a grisly green, unreal.

I see myself step numb under his dead weight,
Christ-like blood on my flanks, his severed head
bouncing against the saddlebags, hailstones
scattered hard as pearls beneath my hooves.
Out of habit, I'll stop when he'd have stopped
and drink when he'd have drunk, imagining
his thighs, the tug on the reins, finding my way
in the dark without him, only the clop of hooves . . .

Thanatos

Schoolgirl vulnerable, still smarting from
the fumbled mismatch of a love affair, I fell
straight out of space and into hell
that night. He was only a voice
on the edge of nothing, but I kept returning
to him, flickering like a stilled film
against the mindless black ferocity of wind.
The roof was trying to suck me out, vast mouth
clamped like a mad baby's over the breast
of a house, whining for milk. I wanted
then to loose my hold, know how it feels
to spiral in the infinite, to Catherine-wheel
across the space that once was love.
Thanatos, pricking at my blood: the truth
that I came searching for, a weariness
that threatened to unclasp my hand, saying
it's over, all over, why resist?
But at the other end of light, the funnelled dark
was a dead body I clung to out of
sheer stubbornness.
                    And the black wind
could not dislodge me from my welding-place,
though its eye bent in and saw me there,
plucked at my white knuckles, severed
the electric umbilical of light. I took
that place and hid it underneath the other times,
less brutal, more arranged. But it comes back,
obliterates that flash between dark and dawn,
and I pretend not to recognise it; call it
desire for solitude. Expurgate, disown the truth.

Heaven, To Be Out There, Under

she might have told him,
not rolling, but holding, taking

the thunder, a wild bird
into shelter, dredging the surf

of the storm, shimmying.
Hell, to be in here, realised,

torn to a stand, stripped
of these leaves, these coverings.

A cold hand summons the star;
warm breath mists the mirror,

repeating the winter,
the dead season, where I

reel from the whirlpool,
the sucking in, the bright mote.

Dragon Woman

She greets you at the door, ordinary enough
in slippers, telephone to her ear.
You only notice the wings later, when they rise
out of her cardigan
like two vast loops of a sea serpent's tail,
ridged and elaborate, mediaeval.

Her smouldering eyes pin you
to the chair. 'Tell me, how did you find me?'
Charred bodies on the news, perhaps,
or those black-singed fumaroles in her front door.
You rest your cup on a scuffed
calf-bound edition of *Paradise Lost*.

You ask about the old days. She looks troubled,
turning her head aside to cough
a thin dusty column of smoke. You pretend
not to notice the bones
stacked up in the hall, her taloned hands
gripping the cup, the ruined parchment
of her throat. You wonder
if that's how you'll end up. 'I'll tell you
what you want to know,'
she says. 'But first, a cigarette.'

The Wife's Lament

a version from the Anglo-Saxon, in memoriam Linda Clayton

I don't belong here, alone in the dark
under these cruel hills. Briars pull
at my clothes where I lie
under an oak all night long, and still
he does not come. Light
burns my feet, so I walk, walk,
walk under this oak, through these caves
of earth, older than grief.
                              Wherever he is,
on the other side of the world perhaps, lost
in ruins under the rain,
he may be calling my name too. Light
falls more sharply where he is.
My lord, my prince, here I must sit
all summer long under this oak,
deep in the earth, rocking with grief.
My sweet, I know you would come
if you could. They broke us apart;
that's why, under this dark hood, I weep.

Year of the Nettle

Delicate green leaves, underside
dusted with poison,
they brushed against my jeans
as I stepped
through swathes of nettles
in the old coppice
under the sallies, the willows.
Even kept clear, my left hand rose
in a mysterious white rash,
knuckle and wrist,
as though imagining contact.
You wandered unscathed,
languid as ever—said
I must have touched one
without noticing.
Yet when our mouths met
that memorable spring,
my lips stung
long after those nettles
in the coppice
had blackened and gone.

In Praise of Cannabis
for Will

How do I love thee? Mainly by inhaling thee
through a tube of ultra-thin paper
finely laced with tobacco, but also
by licking my fingers after crumbling the block
or finding stray skunk on the rug
weeks later, when I've promised myself
no more, and an end to all that.
Yet the smell comes back, like a punch
to the throat, until there's nothing
you can do but go out and score
because there are smokers and then
there are puffers, and even when you're clear
the gear wins, hands down. It's the best prison
in the world, and after a while, all you get is
slightly toasted, and you long for those days
when the animal hit you between the eyes
and your knees refused to move, tingling
with a not unpleasant electric shock.
But now you'd need a monster party spliff
to achieve that kind of damage, and you
must stay straight or you can't keep rolling.
In spite of this, caning is a useful pursuit
for the socially adventurous: you meet
all sorts of interesting dealers and people
who worship animal spirits or use oriental bongs
they picked up in a den in Amsterdam.
But at the end of the day, when most
sane people are tucked up in bed, it's just you
and the beast, and she's so beautiful,
the smoke-haze is nectar, and you drift,
not sleepy, not thinking, but definitely *there*
where everything is manageable, sorted.

Part II

My Mother's Ashes

in memoriam Sheila Holland, aka 'Charlotte Lamb', 1937–2000

My mother was cremated, not buried;
there's no grave,
no plaque on a wall, not even
an urn half-buried
in shrubbery, somewhere
to take my curious children
saying, 'There,
that's where they laid her.'
Instead, she has to be inside here
when I think of her—
that silent waiting room
in the dark of my head—
or up there, like radio waves, invisible
above us, 'crossed over'
rather than dead. Yet
it's disconcerting,
not knowing where my mother is.
Maybe one day I'll find her
at the back of a cupboard,
next to a jar of Seville marmalade
or pickled damsons,
and hold her aloft
in a cracked china pot, saying,
'Look!
My mother's ashes!'

Walks With My Father

My father used to park at Cronk Ny Arrey Laa
and make us tramp
the one and a half thousand feet up there
in thick clinging mist,
falling back with our trousers soaked
and my mother incensed, stuck home
with the Sunday roast. Once
through a fog-drenched cleft in the hills
he led us down to a pebble beach
hundreds of metres below,
twin toddlers and a twelve year old, lost
on the sheer hang of a cliff.
I like to think it was his sense of humour
made him do it. But it was
that sort of place, the Isle of Man,
back in the late seventies.
There were wet slate chasms in the earth
and sheeps' skulls, whitened
by wind, and the grey stone tholtans
of abandoned farms
where a coarse grass shivered over lintels
fallen onto disused paths.
You could lie on your back there
and see the grey sky
through an absence of roof, listen to the wind
finger those broken windows
like hole stops on a flute.
There are few places left like that now,
ranging wild and free,
and no mother to complain. Once
I came home with a frog
in my boot.

A Pair of Boots

On the carpet, leather to
leather, a pair of boots:
one upright, the other unlaced,
recumbent. Both scuffed,
rough from a glancing of mud
like the knees of a child.
Black and tan, like the soft hide
of a spaniel or the deep
wrinkled crease of a Chesterfield,
they wait, abandoned,
restless as soldiers in the half-light,
the one left standing
extending its rictus of leather
to an absent foot.

Whose Hands Were Made of Velvet

He held up his hands
and they were the place of dreams.

Inside each hairy palm, small softnesses of bats
took root, clinging
with astonished intelligent feet
to a skin-space
sweeter than milk.

Gravity

Out there, the island
curves skyward
blue as a whale's back
in the half-light.
Tintagel, royal court
of pearl fishers,
stone sunk
against the blue-black
of mackerel.
In bed, he whispers
how the caves
are dragging it down,
towed slowly
through the centuries
to collapse
like a second Atlantis:
steps oceaned,
towers devoured.
His lips trace
my breasts
blue-veined and round,
and my belly,
thick now with pearls
he hauled
from the wreckage.
Preserve each kiss
my husband warns me;
the world sinks
while we drown gently.

Twins

for Dylan and Morris

We do not know you yet, you are nothing
but bone and fluid and mass to us.
They lift you out through your necklace
of cord, slippery and indignant,
and suddenly you're inspired, all lungs,
pure beetroot. Your brother,
tucked up tight beneath my breast-bone,
does not want to wake. His mild eyes
open in surprise to a world of gowned figures
and white masks.
                            Stitched-up
and emptied from the waist downwards
like a breakfast egg, I lie back
with my arms full of babies. Your father sits
with a perpetual grin on his face
like a man in a Greek comedy.

These lights above the bed are your first stars.
Urgent with milk-haze, you root
for the breast and I gather you in, begin
with your own names.

Warwickshire

Shakespeare's country, they call this;
furthest from the coast

I've ever lived, where a dawn mist
is the closest we come to seascape.

I stand at the kitchen window,
try to imagine water

instead of trees, salt waves
in place of sheep, England

my beleaguered sunken island—
no sign of a peak, only

that thin steely line
they must have seen from the ark

in those languorous days
before the dove came back,

a green twig in her beak.

Fifth

for Indigo

Three days since the blood failed,
and the test turns blue,
a miniature sea between my hands,
nine months to the far horizon.

This must be a girl again, I'm sick
as a drunk all morning
and the world tilts when I walk
like a ship sliding in a bottle.

Twelve weeks and my waist begins
to thicken. I can't hold
anything down, and the boys
are too heavy to carry upstairs.

I meant to stop at two, then three,
then a fourth appeared.
Perhaps I could try hiding
under the covers, or not washing.

This stubborn foot wedged high
under my diaphragm is
more than a fish by thirty weeks:
it's a rich pearl pushing

against an opalescent shell, a poem,
a number, sonic reality;
refusing to be got rid of, cleaving
like a shadow, part of me.

Apples

The horses come here for apples twice a day,
nudging the fence and rubbing themselves
against trees, trampling earth
with their hunters' hooves while they wait.
At first we fed them with palms held flat,
away from the substantial teeth and those warm
brownish lips lifting up to reveal them.
But one always dropped his apple
into white-flowered nettles under the fence
and the other would stoop
to retrieve it, thick sinewy neck supple
as a giraffe's. So now we roll them into the field
or throw them, over-arm, so they bounce
and split soft apple everywhere.
Some days the children are outside playing
and I lift them up, let the baby
grab at a sleek nose with her clumsy fingers
while the boys stare, mesmerised
by the moist brown eyes and those lashes—
like false ones!—seductively curling.
The gentler one comes on his own sometimes,
whinnying and snuffling at the fence.
He turns a wide circle under the horse-chestnut
before moving on, apples
just out of reach and no one in the garden.

Night Voyage

To save the cost of a bed that night
we parked up in a lay-by. Enclosed
in the car as though in an ark
we slept uneasy, restless as animals
under the thick drubbing of rain,
forgetting ourselves in the dark, losing
our voices, even our names.

For years we lay watching as fierce
creatures leapt at our windscreen,
the darkness, the rain—endless it seemed
– surrounding and berating us.

Then a thin light, raw with water,
spoke out of the dark, story upon story,
height upon height, until
the unseen rivers of rain around us rose

and we floated free in our strange barque,
rocking into morning, into light.

Skull of a Bird

God is always in the small
and the wild things. To be part
of that, to mingle
with acorns rotting in the dirt
and a bird's skull,
fragile as paper, is to meet God
and miss him; to hunger
for his music as people hunger
in dark streets, sinew
and bone knotted hard together,
and only stone singing.

Women's Prayer Group, Coventry

The clock on the deanery mantelpiece
has stopped. Outside, a spire
is all that's left
of our medieval cathedral, burnt out
by fire-bombs in the war.
Our group (there are usually eight
or nine of us) meets
each Wednesday for prayer and supper
in an upper room. Here, we set
such ordinary things as childcare, husbands—
our daily bread—
against St. Paul's teachings. How much
should we give to the church?
How much to the poor?
We struggle for words or bore each other
with pettiness. Yet each week
we pray and each week
the clock tells us the same thing: look up!
Bombs are still falling here,
their silent detonations
poised a finger's-breadth above each head,
held off by prayer.

Benediction

                              After
the raised hand of your blessing, I felt
a weight lifted, the dusk
thick with light, humming in the distance
between telegraph poles
                              something
vast and intricate
charging the space in my head
with moths dancing—dust in the beam
and the smudge of a spire
glimpsed above sycamores—
the spirit of the tribe.

Desert Mother

After Fortitude 38 and 39, The Sayings of the Desert Fathers

My cell is the pillar of cloud
where God spoke to Moses.
It's the furnace I stand in,
morning and evening,
an intolerable column of fire
between me and God.

Each day I pack my rucksack, peer out
at the desert. The Sisters
weep for me. Abba Macarius
prays for me. I press
imaginary footprints into the sand,
my hated cell shrinking
in the distance,
nothing but a hot dusty hell
I've crouched in
these seventeen years.

And each night
I lay down my rucksack for a pillow
and praise God
saying, 'Tomorrow, Lord.
Tomorrow.'

Resurrection

When my young daughter clasps
chubby hands
in the small of her back
and parades
from the vegetable patch
to the red shed

I see my mother
at sixty
back from the dead.

Part III

Deciphering the Rejection Letter

Doc Ian
Thankly for these homely carrot honeyful pies.
In rally arry I woolit quit loot ay in—
oh fell I've hit a too lorry.
Plare de sil rue!
Very wisest, Feng Shui.

Door Jam
Thoroughly for these only correct bountiful yams.
I'm roulley army I woubbit quilt fot any is—
al fch I've hid a too loony.
Plane di ail muc!
Very wormey, Frere Lecteur.

Dour Jim
Thankway for these oily concrete lentiful pores.
I'm really angry a rabbit quiet fat again—
if such I'll hole a too lazy.
Please don't send more!
Very worst, In Horror.

Dear Jane
Thank you for these lovely concise? beautiful poems.
I'm really sorry I couldn't quite fit any in—
and feel I've held on too long.
Please do send more!
Very warmest, The Editor.

Cyber Infidelity

Beautiful lover, still beautiful
because unseen, as far apart

as two incalculable griefs
on either side of a war, cast

the broken parts of yourself
over the bridge that separates us —

no less incomprehensible
than history — back into the void

where a limp, or squint, halitosis,
puckered rolls of flesh, a voice

abrupt as a bedspring, can be shed
for this dazzling dive naked

into a fast-as-light vernacular,
cunnilingus of the internet,

fellatio of different parts
of speech — delete, delete, amend —

while the caches of the fluttering ghosts
of our other halves, asleep in bed,

send silent cookies to the heart:
bedtime now, put out the light.

Anal Obsessive

He was a blip on the radar—I had
several that year—but since
he was up front about it—
'Don't trust me, I'm a bastard'—
I let him screw me, and then
screw me. The woman
he left me for was older,
uncompromising, sober.
She would never have rolled over
for that sharp pain
in the derriere, or thought
extensively of England,
face pressed into his mattress
with its bachelor stains
and cute ringlets of pubic hair.
I remember his stubble,
the wind-tunnel tilt of his penis,
how I stripped off for him
the way it's done in Amsterdam—
to be greased up, pokered
and prodded—and can't
imagine now why I bothered.

Books at Auction

i.m. The Little Camel Bookshop

I

I used to arrive early, wander through the clutter:
tables, chairs, a walnut desk
from the nineteenth century, lampstands
and dolls' houses, the usual array of paintings
by artists no one has ever heard of,
bric-a-brac, porcelain dolls with real hair,
a rocking-horse. There was always something odd
to see there, hold upside-down, poke around in
or sit on. I remember polysterene cups,
cheap coffee from the kiosk.
They called me 'love' or 'pet', those men
who humped furniture for a living (in
and out), their stained brown coats
that stank of linseed oil, their cheeky offers
of a cigarette.
⠀⠀⠀⠀⠀⠀⠀⠀I grew muscles
like weeds that year, hefting boxes to the car,
bending my knees. Books, books,
the musty smell of them, like old perfume,
like history—'To H.B. from Lily, 1904',
'To Mother from your Beloved Son George'—
their marbled end-papers foxed, spotted
like trout, the maps and diagrams
that folded out—the entire midship of a schooner
once, in immaculate condition—
the tiny wormholes and the worms themselves
(killed off by freezing overnight).

Though those paper-thin silences
before bidding began
were often like the silences
of our first nights together—eyes meeting briefly,
then lips—love

is not like bidding for books at an auction
(except for the tension
and never being quite sure what
you'll end up with
or how much it might cost you).

II

Books can be like love though,
a high dark dream of love, a secret *only you and I*
can know this love.
So I'd bid more steeply than intended,
burnt up with lust
for some T.S. Eliot First,
then slip outside for a cigarette
empty-handed
and smoke there in the rain. Like Barbara in Brest,
epanouie ravie ruisselante . . .
Yet it was always worth it, at the auction,
buying books in competition. Even
the hours spent on my knees afterwards, bent
over those boxes, sorting out
and cataloguing, pricing up, my hands
book-black by the end of it,
dancing and singing over the covers:

Ha! Ha! Among the Trumpets, Alun Lewis;
Loch Derg from Patrick Kavanagh;
Nil Nil, by Don Paterson, faded blue cloth,
signed by the author, good condition;
Milton's *Paradise Lost*, calf-bound and gilt
in three volumes, 1795;
the *Complete Poems* of Alice Meynell
on hand-made paper, limited numbered edition;
an early *Crow*, slightly foxed,
with marginalia; Vita Sackville-West,
her modest *Selected* from the Hogarth Press;
Betjeman's *Summoned by Bells*, green cloth
minus jacket, a First Edition.

III

Why buy them, to preserve them? Better
to let cyber-space have them, let them be words
on screen, seen and unseen, corruptible.
That page will fade, data disappear, no safer there
than between hard covers,
yet never so beautiful nor dangerous, something real
to hand on, like a name or a sword.

Say that under our fingers, our eyes
or here on the tongue, a book of light is rising:
the word that we made to be heard—dignified
godhead, salt-washed,
bound bone and blood in it,
went to the stake for it, then lost or discarded—
has been hidden from fire, riddled
with worms, pressed and spotted
by browned wild flowers,
over-written by notes scribbled
in margins, recipes
laid down on blank versos and these ghosts
on the flyleaf, the dates and names
of the faithful—when bought, when handed on,
where kept, by whom (though rarely why,
the hidden purposes of readers
blown like dust from gilt-edged spines).

Or rather say, look, this is what we achieved
in our age. This is a book.
Open it to the first page and read.

Night Blue Fruit at the Tin Angel
after The Tunning of Elinour Rumming —*John Skelton (1464?–1529)*

> *'Some wenches come unlaced,*
> *Some housewives come unbraced,*
> *With their naked paps*
> *That flips and flaps'*

Coventry's ringing
and in we come, singing
the tawdry and low
the quick and the slow
both wrinkled and young
with pierced ears and tongue
to give 'em a saga
or swill down the lager
and those who are able
can jump on the table
the strong and the feeble
the poetry people
with 'Give us a song
but don't make it too long'
or 'You've had enough'
and so on, and such
hullaballoo
at the poetry zoo.
All singing and swaying
some of us praying
for that one to stop
or suddenly drop.
Oh, it's smoky as hell
down the Tin Angel
so crowded and tight
on poetry night
folk in the corner
think it's a sauna.
Let's set up a kitty
and drink the whole city.
Let's pull out a plum

and drown us in rum.
Let's watch the girls pass
in short skirts and bras.
Here's plenty of booty
the fat and the fruity
stalking these streets
with their whistles and squeaks
stacking their hips
with ketchup and chips.
Let's pour out the gin
and call 'em all in.
Here's a disco-queen doxy
in search of a taxi
who clippits and creels
in her six-inch heels.
Here's Chelsea and Sharon
Suki and Karen.
Here's Lexi and Carol
they've drunk half a barrel.
Here's Amber and Jade
from down the arcade.
'Who wants to get laid?'
Drooping or drowsy
quick-lipped or lousy
whatever your name
you can read just the same.
This isn't a fight
it's a poetry night.
We've come here to shout
so stand up or get out.
The bolshy and blunt
can read at the front
the rising star
recites at the bar
the talented few

in the queue for the loo
are hopping and cursing
all part of rehearsing.
We gargle and giggle
we fidget and wriggle
and stand in a huddle
our work in a muddle
complain that the mic
is at the wrong height
and could I read two more
or three more or four?
and pick up a suitcase
to bring to the floor.
We're pinching the language
to our best advantage.
We'll take her to bed
both living and dead
with old and new fangles
her tights round her ankles
she's willing, she'll come
for the fiddle and drum
for the pipes and the Klaxon
she's pure anglo-saxon
she's standard, she's foreign
she's leek and she's sporran
she's pidgin and broken
braille and token
she's French and she's Greek
Punjab on the street
she's BBC English
– I've started, I'll finish—
she's Latin, Croatian
she's had every nation
still packing them in
down at the Tin

with a stud in her nose—
it's our olde English rose!
She'll linger and lather
make eyes at your father.
She's British and proud.
You're a hell of a crowd.
Yes, her poets are coming
they're rhyming and humming.
Let's give them a hand
then one for the band
for the Tin Angel crew
and the queue for the loo
that's still going strong
to the end of my song.
Now I'll give up the mic.
I thank you. Goodnight!

IV Boudicca

QUEEN OF THE ICENI

When Prasutagas, leader of the Iceni tribe, died in around
60 AD, his wife Boudicca was flogged by the Romans, her
property seized, and her two daughters raped. In response,
Boudicca raised a vast army of Britons to crush the foreign
settlers. Her brief but excessively violent rebellion ended in
defeat somewhere in the Midlands, after which Boudicca
apparently took poison to end her own life. The Romans were
to remain in control of Britain for another three centuries.

Red Star

They say when I was born
a red star flamed in the east
but it was either torchlight
or the glint of my mother's hair.

They say my first breath
brought the wild geese back
but it was late spring
and the waters were warmer.

They say the great oak split
at the hour of my birth
but it was only lightning
trying to reach earth there.

I saw none of these things
but I've heard them all.
I believe the world trembled
when I started to crawl.

Not Exactly a Virgin

I married Prasutagus in the spring.
We did it the old-fashioned way—
slaughtered everything
and feasted till May.

I remember blossom falling.
He was the stag
and I was the hind
running wild before him.

Prasutagus was a good man
and a better king. I let him
catch me, push me
to the earth, laughing.

There was no pain that day
or in what followed.
In those days, I was less fussy
what I put in my mouth.

I wasn't exactly a virgin
but I hadn't yet seen
a woman's throat ripped out
for refusing to swallow.

Boudicca's Son

They'll tell you
I only gave him daughters

but I had a son once.
For three days.

The pale bluebell of his eyes
closed after sunset

and his whining breath
rattled into silence.

I didn't bother to scream,
or shake him awake.

You get a sense for these things.
Once the soul leaves

there's no calling it back.
I didn't name him.

He wasn't even big enough
to bother burning.

When I went to Prasutagus
and told him the tidings

he simply filled me again
like a bowl of spilt milk.

For days, my breasts ached
under the tight bindings.

The Pleasures of Castration

Prasutagus wasn't even cold yet
and the Roman guard,
a swarm of sandalled bees,
were on us within minutes.

They dragged me out of the crowd
like a whore caught stealing.

One put his hand up my dress,
and by the look on his face
that wasn't all he was planning.

With one blow, I taught him
I don't wear rings because they're pretty.

There was a price for that too.

Even through the blur of his whip
I could hear my girls screaming.

It's strange what little difference
time makes. I still dream
of those men, the pleasures of castration.

Frozen

We pooled out into a field at dawn,
a scattering of angry men
and me, fierce at the heart of them,
my back still wet with blood,
shining from the whip. I was calm,
like water. The pressure of it
frozen. Men, my men. I had those
marks on my bare legs
from damp grass, my bodice
was open, they could see
my breasts. But I was their sister,
their goddess, their queen;
my lightning grief was theirs,
my thunder anger rolled
across the milky fields, a star
for them to follow—on foot
or broken, on their knees.

First Assault

I had to lead the first assault.
They never trust you if you don't.

If I had caught a speeding bullet
in my teeth, they couldn't
have been more impressed.

A black rain of hand-grenades,
men down like dominoes
and there I was, tits out,
hurling an axe round my head,
for all the world
a veteran of ten campaigns.

To be honest
I was bricking myself.

Then my flagman fell.

I caught him on my chest;
I'd had him in my bed
the night before.
Not much to brag about
but nonetheless.

I dropped him to the earth
and sliced the next man
through the throat.

Flashback

Down the scree we skidded
into battle, into combat

and for a moment I was back
in my childhood

chasing the red-haired boy
down the slope
with a whee and a whoop

and a hey ninny, come back,
it was only a joke!

Then the first blow came,
cracking me landlong

but real at least. Here, now.
No longer in the past.

Back in the vicious colliding breath-
knocked-out-of-me present.

A Handful of Bones

They called me 'Boudicca'
the day we took Camulodunum—

'*Victory!*' My moment of fame.

The men thought it was right,
saying I'd lost my old name
the way some girls lose their virginity;
violently, but enjoying the fight.

That night, I rode some man
until he fled, muttering
something about bite marks.

So I sulked in the dark instead,
listening to the rape
of one of the Roman women.

Later, her body was strewn
across my door
like a red carpet, a love token.

Going out, I trod down hard
on her buckled spine.

Found a handful of bones
they'd left unbroken.

The Whole of Britain

Out of Verulamium, we came
to the height of a hill.

I stood and looked down, light
like a weight on my shoulders

and the whole of Britain
glinting before us

like a coin tossed in the sun,
blunt-edged, foreign.

War Games

I lunged out at him,
screaming.

He slammed
a steel-walled chest

against the sway
of my breasts.

I pulped his cheekbones
with an elbow.

He spat blood
on my battledress.

I rammed two fingers
under his eyeball

prising it out
with a pop.

He shrieked the name
of some Roman god

and sank his teeth deep
into my navel.

Afterwards, I wiped
my hands on his hair,

whispered
he was my best ever.

Bewildered Dead

A limping mercenary, half-blind,
took me aside one night
with the blood
still crusted on my arms
and legs—not my blood,
of course, I was better
than that—and said,

'You have to forgive yourself
or they come back.'

I didn't ask what he meant.

Some of the bewildered dead
had already tried that.

Driving the Tribes

We were like a river of mad ants,
unkempt and straggling, huddled
in factions, here one tribe,
there another, not one man on that side
calling this one brother. More men
poured like water
into this flesh-coloured river
at every town, suspicious
of motive, belief, allegiance, honour,
yet still fighting for each other.

For days we ploughed a crooked swathe
through the old valleys,
left them dark, like war paint on dead bodies,
coming upon settlements
smokeless and empty, their folk already gone—
the way you know a storm's coming,
the scent of it on the wind
and those short hairs
on the back of your neck, stiffening.

The chariots, so many chariots, thick dust
clouding the air for hours afterwards,
oak leaves tacky with it, water
greased with it, children
playing in the ruts, women running out
with cloths clamped over their mouths,
skirts raised, to stare at us . . .

Eighty thousand Britons
rending a road where there was none,
working a war-path
from field and cow-shit and bracken.

Headless Woman

They were never expecting us.

Gates were always wide open.
We ate Romans for breakfast
and raped the livestock.
It all got mildly out of hand
after Camulodunum.
Kids murdered, mass graves
stinking behind villas.

Once, I slipped on a brain
in the road: decapitated owner
half-lying, half-sitting
against the ruins of her house.

I couldn't help laughing;
she looked so comical,
feet dragged in the dirt,
spare head grinning.

War Paint

Some of the men went naked into battle
except for their war paint—

it was like watching gods fight,
blue-thighed, hanging like horses,

like a dog after a bitch,
with their own blood in their eyes,

sweat on their hands,
mud past their ankles, their knees,

flies on their shoulders
and the crow in full sun afterwards

unspooling their innards.

Ghost Light

Perhaps it was crouched
among the trees, down in the wet
as a child, knees bent
under the fierce slap of the wind,
the cold shoulder of the wind,
the get-out-I-can-handle-it wind

that these plans—unknown,
half-formed, yet firm
as bone, unchangeable as earth—
first came. Eight years old
and a woman already,
by thirty a warrior.

I never wanted Prasutagus dead.

Yet dead he is. And here's
my chance to bury grief
with him, draw on my forehead
with ashes, dance
in the ghost light of his absence
as I was always meant
to dance, a spear in my hand.

Strong Hands

There was a man after Londinium
who could have meant something

if he hadn't fallen at Verulamium,
shot in the groin at point-blank range.

Darius, his name was,
and he had strong hands.

Sometimes, when the sod inside me
showed no sign of finishing,

I would dream about Darius

and come like a wild bitch
howling all the way.

Darius had that effect on me.

Purification

It had been raining for weeks—
or that's how it felt to us,

rain like a sluice through the trees
bright-gold under it—the sun

hefting up afterwards
as it used to do in my childhood

prickly and golden
over the drowned black drub

of a thicket, a spinney
where we stood by steaming horses

and make-shift tents, impatient
for the rain to finish

rinsing the blood off, to purge us
for death and be done with it.

History

There were moments when, standing tired
on some such hill or other,
I could see the whole of things spread out
across the fields, everything
that had happened, there in clear weather
and making sense at last, like the thin fingers
of withy woven in a fence,
like loosened threads drawn back together
in a pattern; not mine,
nor theirs, but something in between.
Now it seems more like death,
like the end of everything.
                          And yet,
we've done all this before, danced
in the black heat of history,
the burnt remains of history,
high on the steppes, the dry plains,
danced on the seas, on the arctic winds,
in our old clothes and our new clothes,
using unfamiliar words, each day
another journey into death, each night
this tiny sweating dance of love,
learning where all the patterns start
and end, where history begins.

Last Stand

The woods above were thick
with sniper fire. Below
Romans bludgeoned faces
with rifle butts
and steel-capped elbows,
crushed our dying men
as they advanced
and broke the man-wall
down in waves.
             In the end,
they got me out
before I had a chance to fight.

I still remember looking back,
dazed with sunlight,
song-thrush piping blithely.

Doppelgänger

I stripped and dipped
my face to the river
but caught the goddess there
in her white mirror,

a raven perched
on the shrug of her shoulder,
that bird who loves
to pick men clean.

Her skin was pale
and her glorious hair
a cold flame
dancing on the water.

I stared into her eyes.
Boudicca. Andraste.
She whispered "War itself
is the enemy."

I touched her face
and let it swim.
That was the last thing
she said to me.

Magpie

They captured us at first light, curled up asleep
outside the crater of a town.

They executed my bodyguard. I had to watch them
clubbed to death.

They chopped my fiery waist-length hair
that Prasutagus loved.

The grass was damp. I slipped once,
hands bound, mist surging
over all Britain.
                    On my knees
through the sun glare
out of the heart of an oak
I saw a magpie
flash its tail and fly.

Suicide

In the end, they had to use a crowbar
on my teeth, force the poison in.

They didn't even bother raping me.

After the first breath, I was high
on mercury, lungs pure silver.

I was radioactive; they could have
found me in the dark. How Suetonius,
that fat Roman dumpling,
must have laughed. The end
was confused. Some screaming, vomit.
It hurt, I know that much.

Nothing else. Just good British dirt
and closing my mouth on it.

Printed in the United Kingdom
by Lightning Source UK Ltd.
115067UKS00001B/193-216